1925

1925

The Depression, the War, Abandonment and My Life

JUNE HEALY HEIDT

ISBN: 1511977361
ISBN 13: 9781511977364
Library of Congress Control Number: 2015907051
CreateSpace Independent Publishing Platform
North Charleston, South Carolina

This book is dedicated to

Lois Healy Knobel
and
Robert Charles Placious.

We are the last three from 987.

ACKNOWLEDGMENTS

Thank you to Edward R. Heidt (CSB) and Ruthanne Heidt-Jennings, who made this book happen.

Thank you to my readers:

Arlene Knobel Bobin
Peggy Grove Douglas
Bobbi Grove Jeffery

Thank you to Robert Joseph Placious for the pictures from your dad's collection.

CONTENTS

PREFACE

When my sister Ruthanne first started this project a few years ago, I thought that she was undertaking a daunting, time-consuming, Herculean task. Gathering and reading through our ninety-year-old mother's notes and stories and shaping them into a coherent narrative seemed to me to be on the level of a PhD project. In addition to reading Mom's notes and stories and sifting through her memories, Ruthanne also wanted the memoir to have photos. So she and Mom began the arduous process of looking through Mom's many boxes of photos along with an ongoing addition of new photos from cousin Robert Placious's father's collection. The project appeared overwhelmingly complex, frustrating, and exhausting—to me, anyway. I remained at the periphery until Ruthanne produced a workable version, which she sent by e-mail to Mom and me for proofreading and editing. When I received and started reading what they had put together, I was utterly amazed. I found the story readable, interesting, and coherent, and as a student of autobiography for most of my academic life, I like to think I am being objective. But, of course, as the son of the subject, I am indeed not.

Then the time came for publishing. After putting the text before other sets of eyes—cousins Arlene, Peggy, and Bobbi, who are themselves excellent readers and editors—we ended the search for a publisher by signing on with CreateSpace.

What emerged is truly amazing and worth reading. Mom was a child of the Depression of 1929, a young adult during World War II, and a survivor of abandonment by her father; her story resonates beyond family and friends. I am very proud of what Mom experienced and how she and Ruthanne have pieced the stories together to form her story. Oddly enough, Ruthanne is a catalyst for many projects like this, going back to 1982, when she made contact with our grandfather (Mom's father) and motivated our first and only reunion with him. I encourage the reader to jump into these pages of great stories. I personally see the trip to Belfast and Mom's meeting with her long-gone father as stories that could stand on their own as plays or movies—not to mention the description of the 1929 Depression and how it affected Mom's upbringing.

My own PhD dissertation was an autobiography and memoir, and I taught a course on the subject for many years at Saint Thomas More College in Saskatoon, Saskatchewan, Canada. I particularly enjoy how people represent themselves in their storytelling, where the line between fiction and nonfiction, truth telling and lying, is cleverly disguised and manipulated, oftentimes unbeknown to the author. And I found this process particularly fascinating in my mother's retellings not just of her own experiences but particularly of her experiences that included me, though I realize I have a different point of view.

I think one of the secrets behind autobiographies and memoirs is the fact that the stories are told from the unique point of view of the individual as author. If the stories are yours, you can narrate them the way you remember them. Truth is not necessarily at stake, but your version of the truth is. My dissertation director, Jay Martin, once said to me that autobiographies and memoirs have proliferated and become very popular (especially among those in the public eye) because the public is fascinated with the private lives of other people. We like watching each other.

Last but not least, I think this is a distinct opportunity for my mom to recapitulate and reenvision her life. She offers her perspective and voice to readers who may have a similar courage within them, who might be coming to a sense of ending about some aspect of their lives. Storytelling and narration are ways of recovering and integrating what is the author's and no one else's. In the process of telling stories, the stories of one's life are integrated into a whole cloth of the person's life. "Integrate" means that the stories do not stand alone as isolated, incoherent, disjointed bits of confusion but instead come together to form a life that means something to the person who gives voice to them.

In the process of writing and collecting your stories, you may find yourself asking, what have I done with my life? Or, why did that happen to me? Forming these stories into a memoir can assist in answering these questions. The painstaking process of collecting and writing is more important than the end product. The day-by-day journey outweighs the destination when significance, impact, and meaning are being created. "Are we there yet?" and "How much longer?" give way to "How am I present in what I am doing right now?" The irony of writing a memoir is that writers can go to past moments and make them what they want. Individuals can learn to be present in the moments as they pass. There is no real concern about the future because the writers will be present to those moments when they arrive. Walter Horatio Pater, a nineteenth-century British essayist and literary critic, once said, "Art comes to you proposing frankly to give nothing but the highest quality to your moments as they pass." Hence, you must ask, "What brings the highest quality to my moments as they pass?"

In Robert Bolt's play *A Man for All Seasons*, there is an interesting interchange between Thomas More and his son-in-law, Richard Rich.

"Why not be a teacher?" Thomas says to Richard. "You'd be a fine teacher. Perhaps—a great one."

Richard responds with, "And if I was, who would know it?"

The wise Thomas says, "You, your pupils, your friends, God—not a bad public, that. Oh, and a quiet life."

Edward Heidt
May 2015

ONE

MY GRANDPARENTS

Frank J. Vetter

My maternal grandfather, Frank J. Vetter, was born March 16, 1864, in Germany. To avoid conscription,

Frank left Germany in 1881 when he was just seventeen years old. He did not want to enter into the army. Frank left his mom, dad, and brother, whose name was Rudolf, in Germany.

Before the major waves of German immigration began, already 8.6 percent of the US population was German. Many had immigrated to Pennsylvania seeking religious freedom or had come under the redemptioner system, which provided German peasants free passage to America but indebted them to a businessman from four to seven years to repay the cost of the voyage. In the 1880s, 1.4 million Germans immigrated to the United States. German Christmas traditions provided the model for many of the American Christmas traditions, including the giving of gifts, the Christmas tree, and the emphasis on family. German immigrants strengthened the labor movement. Albert Einstein, the prominent physicist, was a German immigrant. Baseball legends Babe Ruth and Lou Gehrig were both sons of German immigrants.

After arriving in New York City, Frank left the ship to sit on a rock and watch the ship sail away. He knew little English, and his travels through the state of New York led him to find a home in Rochester, New York. I imagine Grandfather Frank had made some contact with Germans already living in Rochester. At that time, foreigners who came to America usually settled in German, Jewish, or Polish communities, depending on their nationality. Thank God that is no longer true. I am happy to say that we have reached a time where our society is attempting to look for common ground rather than focusing on differences.

Grandfather Frank—or "Pa," as the family called him—made one trip back to Germany sometime before my birth in 1925, likely in 1923. Pa had a family picture taken to show his relatives in Germany.

Top row: Frank Vetter, Charles McCarthy, Huldy Vetter, William Vetter, Mary Vetter, Harold Healy, Joseph Placious

Second row: Eva Clancy Vetter; Gertrude Vetter McCarthy, holding Emily; Frank J. Vetter; Emily Vetter Healy, holding Lois; Anna Vetter Placious, holding Robert and Raymond

Sitting: Joseph W. Placious and Helen A. Placious Grove

Pa met and married my grandmother, Mary Maier, who was born October 14, 1863. They met in Rochester, New York[1] in 1887. She died of nephritis at the age of fifty-six on July 2, 1919. Grandmother Mary was the only child of Hugo

---

1 http://www.rochesterhistory.org/
http://www.cityofrochester.gov/175/
http://www.rochestergerman.com/history/index.html

Maier, who was born in Germany, in 1838 and died in 1905. Mary's mother, Katrina Gunkel Maier, was born in 1839. My great-grandmother Katrina came to America in 1866 when she was twenty-seven years old. She died in 1922 of old age at eighty-three. Katrina's headstone reads "Catherine." When my grandparents arrived in America, they became Americanized and spoke English instead of German. Katrina may have changed her name to Catherine because she wanted a more American-sounding name, though I'm not really sure about that.

TWO

987

All of my memories of growing up take place at 987 Clifford Avenue in Rochester, New York. We nicknamed the house "987." I remember such happy times there, though there were also some very difficult times.

Grandmother Mary liked to put her apron on in the morning and keep it clean and white until she took it off at the end of the day. Her mom lived right there at 987 Clifford Avenue with her. Katrina took over most of the daily duties for her daughter. We would joke that Mary must have been spoiled.

Mary loved to play the piano. In fact, that piano was played for many years in our reception hall at 987 by Aunt Anna Placious, my mom's oldest sister. I can remember

Sunday afternoons when we would ask Aunt Anna to please play the piano. Aunt Anna kept the sheet music in the piano bench. We would go through the music and pick our favorite songs for her to play, making sure to get all of the songs we wanted to hear so Aunt Anna wouldn't have to keep getting up. Some favorites included "Let Me Call You Sweetheart," "When Your Hair Has Turned Silver," "Down by the Old Mill Stream," and so many others. We would all gather around the piano and sing while Aunt Anna played. This is such a joyful memory for me.

Mary and Pa had seven children. Anna Vetter Placious was the first, born July 17, 1888. She died May 18, 1958, at the age of seventy. Aunt Anna suffered many years with high blood pressure. William was born next, whom I didn't know very well, and then Frank, who died in infancy. The fourth child was again named Frank. Huldy, born June 30, 1894, died of a heart attack on August 30, 1964, when she was seventy years old. Huldy was born with a condition called anencephaly that affected the development of her skull and brain. Therefore, her mind did not exceed the age of twelve or thirteen.

Gertrude was born January 17, 1898, and died following a lengthy illness in January 1985 when she was eighty-seven. Gertrude had adult-onset diabetes that ultimately took her sight. On January 14, 1899, my mother, Emilia- also known as "Emily", was born. She died of leukemia on December 9, 1959, when she was sixty years old.

Emily, Anna, and Gertrude Vetter

Four sisters: Emily Healy, Huldy Vetter,
Gertrude McCarthy, Anna Placious

Pa sold his first house on Clifford Avenue to a young doctor named Howard Burns. Dr. Burns was our family doctor for years. When I was a child, doctors would come directly to the home when someone was sick. I retained Dr. Burns as our family doctor after I married. Once, my oldest son, Edward, fell and cut his head above the left eye. I just stopped the bleeding and waited for Dr. Burns to arrive. By the time he got there, the cut had already started to heal, so he decided against stitches. Of course, Ed still reminds me of that occasion every so often by looking at me and pointing at the tiny scar.

Joe and Anna Placious, 1927

Pa's new home at 987 Clifford was planned according to his specifications. Pa also purchased a duplex on Durnan Street, just a few blocks away. Pa rented out the duplex to tenants.

He became a butcher and opened his own store on Portland Avenue. I'm not sure what his education was in the butcher line; it might have been trial and error in those days. My thoughts are that perhaps his father had been a farmer. When Pa was a boy, they lived inland in Germany, so their livelihood was from the land. Pa did love farms.

Sawdust was always on the floor of a meat market. Most likely it helped keep the store sanitary. I don't remember the name of Pa's market—maybe Frank's Market or Vetter's Market. I remember shuffling my feet around in the sawdust. That was Pa's livelihood until he retired and his son William continued the business.

Aunt Anna was a buttonhole maker. She worked in a tailor shop until she married Uncle Joe. Uncle Frank became a chemist at Kodak. Aunt Gert made ties. When Aunt Gert resigned to get married, she continued to make the ties at home for a while. Emelia inspected cameras at Kodak until she retired.

When Emelia entered first grade, the teacher announced, "There are too many Emelias in this class." The teacher pointed to my mom and told her that from now on she would be known as Emily. I can't imagine a parent today allowing such a change. From that day forward, my mom was known as Emily. I didn't learn about her baptized name until I found out from my cousin Emily McCarthy in 2008. We all called her Emily and did not even know about the change.

Uncle Frank, World War I

All of the children in my family took music lessons. Aunt Anna and Aunt Gert played the piano, and Mom played the violin. When I was a child, we didn't have money for music lessons. My friend Myra had an aunt who taught dancing lessons for fifty cents. I could not afford to pay, but she would let me watch.

Pa was considered well off until the 1929 Depression. When Grandmother Mary died in 1919, Pa asked his daughter Anna and her husband, Joe, if they would consider selling their first home on Spiegal Park. Pa needed their help to care for Huldy, Anna's challenged sister. His mother-in-law, Katrina, was living with him as well. So Anna and Joe agreed to return to 987. They had two children at that time, Helen and Joseph. The twins, Bob and Ray, hadn't been born yet.

Aunt Gert and my mom were twenty and twenty-one years old, respectively, when Grandmother Mary, their mom, died in 1919. They were both working full-time jobs. Katrina helped out with Huldy and the great-grandchildren, Helen and Joseph. Helen was Katrina's pride and joy and received much love and attention. Helen and Joseph were the only grandchildren at that point, so they received attention from two unwed aunts, Gert and Emily, as well as from Mother and Father. I often wonder how Helen and Joe felt about my sister and me moving in when Helen was thirteen and Joe was ten. Helen was coming into her own independence. We were both younger than five, and my sister, Lois, agreed with me that Helen, just entering her teen years, probably wasn't too happy with the situation. But we grew and learned to share our lives and love each other very much. As adults with our own families, we spent many vacations and visits together.

But now I've jumped ahead a bit.

Pa designed and built 987. This home was a warm, loving, kind, and safe place to be. Many, many people visited 987, and they always felt welcomed. We still talk about 987 today, even though it is long gone. It was my home, my beginning. I'll be forever grateful that I was surrounded by loving, kind people in my childhood home. It represented a safe haven.

It was my castle, filled with people who loved me and took care of me. In many ways, 987 had a strength all its own that protected us.

Our home, 987, was so special to anyone who visited. You can see the license in this photo.

Uncle Joe Placious got a license plate that read MN987. After he died, Helen's husband, Al, acquired the plate number and then gave it to his daughter, Peggy, for her first car.

THREE

HULDY

Huldy worked around the house for Pa and Grandmother Mary. Huldy was very capable. She would frequent a couple nearby stores to buy candy. Huldy would stand in front of her father with her hand held out, and he would place a nickel in her hand. Off she would go to purchase some candy. If she found peanuts in the candy, she would blame the storekeeper for selling it to her. She would say, "He must know I can't eat nuts."

Penny candy was plentiful in those days. For one cent you could get two or three bolsters of Mary Janes, Green Leaves, BB Bats (a long taffy sucker), and many others. These were some of my favorites.

Every day Huldy would take her father's lunch to him at the butcher shop. The walk took her thirty minutes, and she had to cross a couple streets. Since there was no refrigeration, Huldy would take his lunch fresh from home. Pa knew Huldy liked to bring him his lunch. She loved her dad, and he was always considerate of her. Pa was so gentle and kind to Huldy. I never remember him ever raising his voice to anyone or over anything.

When I was home from school ill, Huldy would sit on my bed and tell me stories. She loved to talk about black veils and holy cards. She would bring out all of her black veils and tell me where she wore them and for what occasion. She kept all of her holy cards neatly stacked in boxes. She would talk about the people who died and remembered them all. She would very carefully fold the cards back into the boxes after telling her stories. My memory of Huldy, in spite of her mental disability, was that she was always kind and comforting to me.

Huldy continued to share her stories with others. My oldest son told me that she invited him to her wedding and piano recital. He often wondered if her stories were real. I explained to him that Huldy would hear us talking about going to recitals or weddings. Huldy would repeat stories she heard other people tell and she would appropriate them to herself. Huldy was a careful listener as we talked about what was for dinner, what we wore, or who was there. She would make the stories her own. When Huldy was at an adult home in her later years, the ladies there told me they loved her stories.

Huldy would often incorporate dishes in her stories. We had everyday dishes as well as good dishes that we used only on Sundays or holidays. We had a local movie theater called the Dixie Theatre that created a "dish night" once a month. A free dish was given out to all who attended the movie that night. Aunt Anna would purchase an adult ticket for me so I could get a dish too, to help complete the set. When the movie was over, you could hear dishes breaking as people got up, forgetting the dishes were on their laps. I was very careful to hold on to my plate for Aunt Anna during the movie before we made the long, cold walk home.

Huldy looked after all of us. We were a family of eleven at 987. The boys, sometimes referred to as the twins, had paper routes. Huldy would be at the side door when they would arrive home to hold the door open so they could bring their bicycles in and wipe them off if it had rained.

Sometimes when I was walking with Huldy, the passing cars would slow down to look at her because of her under-sized head. Huldy would ask me, "What are they looking at?" I knew people looked at Huldy quizzically. The fact that they might be making fun of her broke my heart. Because of her small head, she did look different. People staring at her would sometimes anger me. I would ask them, "What are you looking at?" I knew Huldy to be kind and thoughtful with a heart only filled with love.

When I was in kindergarten, Huldy would walk to the public school to pick me up when I would fake illness to go home early. The Catholic school didn't have kindergarten, so I went to public school. My sister and cousins would have off on holy days, and I wanted to be home with them.

Huldy could get riled up. At Christmas time our parents created a tradition. They would close the doors to the living room, where Santa was decorating the tree. Huldy would be doing the supper dishes. We were children and excited to see what Santa left all of us. We would ask Huldy to hurry because Santa was there. She would forcefully say, "He can wait." Santa was not there when we went in, just the presents. This was generally done on Christmas Eve at 987. On Christmas Day, my mom, Lois, and I would travel to Belfast, New York, to visit my brother, Bill, who was raised by my father's parents.

Grandmother Mary's mother, Katrina, taught Huldy German and took her to church. I believe there would be a place in a school for Huldy today. I believe she would have had her own dishes, held a job, and perhaps even lived in a group home. I thank God for science and research because that is what helps so many challenged people do so much more to enjoy their life. I wouldn't trade one moment of my life with Huldy. She taught me compassion. She taught me simple abundance. Her heart was so full of grace and love. I'm the lucky one. We must always remember to give of our bounty to help the poor, to help those not gifted with special, caring parents and positive influences. I learned that from Aunt Huldy.

FOUR

EMILY AND GERTRUDE

When my mom and her sister Gertrude were married at a double wedding ceremony on April 25, 1922, in Holy Redeemer Church, Pa stopped renting out the duplex on Durnan so they could move there. Gertrude and her husband, Charles, lived upstairs. My parents lived downstairs. At some point, Pa gave Aunt Gert and Uncle Charlie some money to purchase a farm. I have learned that they were told to pay it back to my mother. Years later their eldest daughter, Emily, named after my mother, told me how pleased Gert and Charlie had been when they fulfilled that obligation.

Aunt Gert and Uncle Charlie found a farm they liked on Freshhauer Road in Shortsville, New York. Pa loved to visit to the farm. I do believe this love of the farm was in his blood from childhood. Our families gathered for many picnics at the farm. I loved to go there. They had so many animals in the barn. We could watch as cows were milked, and they always warned us about the bull. He was a mean one, I guess. I never took any chances. With so much open ground we could play baseball. My mother and Aunt Gert were only one year apart and enjoyed being together.

Front row: Harold and Emily Healy,
Gertrude and Charles McCarthy
Back row: Leland Healy and Frank Vetter

After only three years, my parents' marriage was failing. On the night of my birth in 1925, my father was nowhere to be found. I barely remember my father. When I was two years old, he deserted us. My older sister, Lois, remembers him and how he hurt our mom. Mom put out a warrant for his arrest, to help support us, but he was never found.

Today, I am sure he would be found, and we would have received support from his paycheck. Because he wasn't there for us, we had to get help from our family. We moved to 987 with Aunt Anna, Uncle Joe, Pa, Huldy, Helen, Joe, and the twins, Bob and Ray. When my brother, Bill, was born, he was given to my paternal grandparents in Belfast, New York. My mom had to work full-time so she could help pay for food, rent, and so forth. She never got to be a stay-at-home mom for us. She was a very responsible parent—I never felt slighted by her absence, but I think she might have missed being at home with us.

So, 987 came to our rescue. It was Anna and Joe's home with their four children, along with Pa and Huldy. Now Mom, Lois, and I entered this secure home, making us a unique three-family unit. Upstairs were four bedrooms, a bathroom, and a second stairway to the attic. One bedroom was Anna and Joe's. Another was Pa's. Another was Helen's. My mother, Lois, Huldy, and I occupied the fourth bedroom. Anna and Joe's three boys, Joe, Bob, and Ray, set up a separate, enclosed room in the attic. Our home was our safe haven, and the respect and love we all felt for each other as a family enabled us to get along so well.

Sometimes, deep in my heart, I believe we were better off without our father. However, the consequences were great. I find forgiving him difficult because we had to be separated from our little brother. Someone once said to me, "Don't let anyone live in your brain rent free." There is no future without forgiveness. God forgives anyone who asks for it. I believe that too. My dad never asked me for forgiveness.

I met him before he died. But I think it may have been more for his benefit than mine, my sister's, or my brother's. I didn't know anything about my father or his life. He never really fathered me. He failed to love us the way we needed growing up.

This letter is re-typed from the hand-written original. Therefore, punctuation, spelling and grammar remain in the letter to my father from his Aunt Lizzie regarding him marrying my mom:

Ithaca, NY Wed 1922pp
My dear Harold

To-days mail brought me your letter and I like you had thought before now I would have a letter written to you. Well you and I have the intentions and am sure understand if no one else does.

Yes Laddie your invitation came to me all right and Marys I sent to her. Now I may not be able to express to you all I feel for as you say we are so often misunderstood. But I want you to know that my heart is too full of good wishes for you to express them in words either written or said. You have I know given this step you are about to take due consideration and advise or council from me is not needed. May Gods richest blessing on you and she whom you have chosen as you stand before His altar on the morning of the twenty-fifth. May there never come a time in your life when worldly affairs dim your vision to your first duty. I am so glad to have known Emily and so glad you have known her. There is no life happier then the married life if each strive to do the best for each other. And that is no hard or heavy task when your interests are one. My boy let me assure you it has been and is a very great disappointment to your mother that I can not go there, there are so few of us I wish we might have all been there to wish you God-speed. It has been to her an awful hurt that mother had to go and who had she been spared would surely have been with you on the morning of your wedding. Let it be our belief and consolation that we think of her as knowing of the things that are happening to those she loved best and whose interests were ever first in her mind. Your mother has said she could not tell how many times in the few months before she left us she expressed a wish that you two boys might do well for yourselves. And that you might choose wisely. Twas a sorrow to her that some of our relatives had made mistaken marriages. No Harold I never for a moment have given it a thought that you were doing aught that was wrong in marrying at this time. We can not harm those gone before us. If on next Tuesday morning as you stand as I believe you will very close to God as you take the marriage vows you can for a moment let your thoughts go to the beyond let your soul utter a prayer for the two grandmothers who were they kneeling in the church with you would be most sincere in praying for Gods blessing to rest on you both. You will ere the week is over hear from me again and if in the weeks to come I can get you any thing you want along the same line let me know at any time. Measure not my little gift by size or value. But as I stated at the beginning from the bottom of my heart I wish you both a long life full to the brim and over flowing with love health and happiness. You can not have full measure of the first without the last I shall always be glad to hear from you and perhaps some time when it comes right you will come to Ithaca.

Lovingly and always
Aunt Lizzie
R.R. 2, Ithaca, NY

FIVE

MEETING MY FATHER IN 1982

I was fifty-seven when I met my father for the first time. It was 1982. He was eighty-two. I had absolutely no feelings for him, though I do feel grateful for good genes from both of my parents. I am grateful for my life. My health is good.

We learned of my father's address, and my daughter Ruthanne contacted him. I still remember when she called me; I was at work. I knew she had written a letter to him. She said, "Guess who I just talked with," and I said, "My father." She said she was planning a trip to Florida where he lived. She said she wanted to meet him and why didn't I join her. Lois's daughter, Mary Ann, lived in Florida and welcomed us to stay with her.

My children and I flew to Florida to meet this man. We called him and made arrangements to meet him at his home. He lived in a mobile home park. My father was delighted to meet me and some of his grandchildren. He and his wife welcomed us into their home. He had remarried after the death of my mother in 1959. We asked him why he did what he did so many years ago. He simply replied that he was a dumb young man. He also made some comment about the family all speaking German, which he didn't know, and that they'd rather clean the house than go out to a party.

He still held ill feeling for his own mother. I told him that she raised his son when he left us and that Bill was a fine young man. Harold's answer to me was that his mother must have learned something.

He never apologized or commented on his own negligence. He told me that he knew we'd be taken care of. I did not say it to him, but I feel it is a father's responsibility to take care of his children.

My son remembers him saying that we did all right without him. My son later told me that he too wanted to say that, yes, Lois, Bill and I did all right, but your leaving affected the way I raised my children. I was always ensuring that the doors were locked in the evening after dinner—so no one could escape! My fear of abandonment ran deep.

I know my father was genuinely pleased to see his children. Later my sister, Lois, and brother, Bill, met him in April 1983.

June of 1983 was the first time I had ever sent a Father's Day card. After sitting through all my school years watching classmates write out cards, draw pictures, and send spiritual bouquets to their dads, I finally got to send a card to my father.

Finding a Father's Day card wasn't easy because my father hadn't done any of the things written on the cards. Nonetheless, we each sent him a card. He had been regularly writing letters since we met, and when I didn't get an acknowledgment for the card, I called his home. His wife's sister answered. Harold Healy had died of a heart attack on June 14, 1983, before receiving any of our Father's Day cards. She said his wife was not feeling well and not to call again.

Perhaps she feared we'd seek some inheritance. We never would have done that. I'm not sure he had much to give anyhow. He lived in a mobile home with an old car in the driveway. When he was with my mom, he was an auto mechanic. I suppose he could have received a good wage if he had stayed with it.

In the end, I believe that when my sister, brother, and I visited him, we gave him closure for what he did to us; however, he died before receiving any of our Father's Day cards.

SIX

HARD TIMES INCLUDED HAPPINESS

Emily Healy; Anna Placious, holding Joseph
Placious; Gertrude McCarthy; Joe Placious; Mary
Vetter; Katrina Gunkel Maier; Huldy Vetter

Little girl in front: Helen Placious Grove

Because of my father's choices, Aunt Anna and Uncle Joe lost their independence. They agreed to add three more to the eight people already living at 987.

It was a large, lovely home with a full basement and large attic. There were four bedrooms, a hall, and a full bathroom upstairs. The main floor had a big kitchen, dining room, pantry, living room, reception hall, and a very large closet. We each had a hook on which to hang our only coat. A single staircase to the second floor had access on stairways from both the kitchen and the reception hall.

Ray Placious, June and Lois Healy, Bob Placious

The family often kidded that the numerous children arriving for Aunt Gert and Uncle Charlie probably scared my father away. Aunt Gert had Emily in 1923, Norma in 1924,

Meryl in 1925, and Joyce in 1926. Charles followed, and then Jane, Elna, Monica, and Richard. My father was long gone in 1927, so he didn't even know about the others. My mom was pregnant with her third child, my brother Bill, in 1927.

Uncle Charlie said my mom went back to 987 and spent too much time there during her marriage. I don't know about any of that, and I didn't understand the joke about Aunt Gert and Uncle Charlie having so many children so quickly. I was hurt because my father deserted us. He deserted me.

June Healy

I believe my family and I received our strength through the Catholic Church. Even the Catholic Church says you do not have to live with someone if the situation is not good. He could have left my mother, but how could he have left his children? I was only two years old, Lois was four, and Bill wasn't even born yet.

No Catholic ever thought of divorce or separation of any kind. No Catholic would just run away, leaving the spouse to wonder where their partner is. My father was obviously unhappy in his marriage and wanted some kind of divorce or separation. Instead of saying that, he just left. We were shocked by something totally unexpected. The Catholic Church, however, also taught us about accepting suffering like Jesus did: follow in Jesus's footsteps and suffer like He did. This experience indeed caused deep suffering for us, and the church's teaching was a tremendous help. The church says we are to forgive our enemies and those who hate us—as Jesus did on the cross—"Father, forgive them, for they know not what they do." I never remember my mother saying anything bad about my father. She just said, "He is the one who is missing out." So once we had come to grips with the fact that my father was actually gone, the church's teaching helped us. My mother never remarried or dated because she believed her marriage to my father was indissoluble. And I don't know if she ever forgave him, but she never spoke ill of him.

As members of the human race and creatures of God, I think we all should seek God, be faithful to Him, and recognize Jesus Christ and how He saved us through His death on the cross. I strongly believe we are the church that has been handed down through Scripture and tradition, from which many churches broke off. The Catholic Church has much dissension, but Christ always promised to stay with us. He gave us free will to choose. We are not puppets that He controls. We have to recognize Him on earth so He will recognize us in heaven.

In 1927 that was not easy to do. Divorce was not accepted socially, not to mention religiously, at that time. There was no welfare or social security. But I thank God that Pa and Aunt Anna and Uncle Joe graciously welcomed my mother, sister, and me into their home at 987. They themselves had a family with my cousins, Helen, Joe, Bob and Ray, and Huldy. Aunt Anna was the oldest of six children. I am sure she had many duties as the eldest. She sadly expressed to my mother that taking care of a new baby would be difficult, if not impossible, for her. I believe Aunt Anna suffered the most; she had extremely high blood pressure. She looked tired, and her eye twitched continuously.

Mom asked her brother Bill and his wife, Mary, if they would take my brother until he started kindergarten. Aunt Anna said he could move in once he started school. They refused. I cannot remember why, although, in my later years, I thought it was odd that Mom would name her son Bill. My grandmother's father's name was Bill, so maybe my brother was named after him. I don't recall asking about it or anyone telling any stories regarding my brother's name. I do remember Mom telling me that the doctor said I was a June baby, being born in June. Had the doctor not said this to my mother, I would have been called Bridget.

My brother, William Charles, was born on April 13, 1928; it was a Friday the thirteenth. Bill was sent to Belfast, New York, some eighty miles away, to be cared for by my father's parents.

My paternal grandfather, Henry DeForest Healy, was born in 1874 and died of cancer on April 24, 1944, at the age of seventy. My paternal grandmother, Anna Fox Healy, was born in 1875 and died in 1950 at the age of seventy-five from cancer of the esophagus.

Gramma Healy's doctor had wanted her to go to Roswell Cancer Center in Buffalo, New York, but she refused. Her money was dwindling, and she felt she had just enough to last until her death. She was a very strong woman with a set of rules and boundaries she believed in and followed. I remember close to her death all she could eat was melted ice cream because she had difficulty swallowing. My mom took time off from work and cared for her in the Belfast home for about four weeks. By that time, my brother had returned to Rochester to attend the Rochester Institute of Technology. He would return to Belfast every weekend to help Mom with Gramma. At the time, my sister and I were married and busy caring for our own families.

I loved Gramma Healy, but she was stern. She was tall and slim. She always walked with her head up and carried a positive, proper posture. Once, Gramma wanted me to have a bath, and I refused. Lois had had her bath and received Fireman's Hat candy, which was a piece of chocolate shaped like a fireman's hat with cream inside. I am sure I ended up getting a bath, but I don't remember receiving a chocolate. I remember Bill once saying that if he complained about something, Gramma would say, "There's the door."

Life was not a game to Gramma. Life was serious, and she had to overcome many odds. Her own father, William Fox, was born in 1844 and died at the age of fifty-six in 1900, the year my father was born. I was told that my great-grandfather was an alcoholic, and Gramma's husband was what people called "a drinker" in those days. So was her son, my father.

She graduated normal school, which is what a teacher's college was called—not college, but normal school. My brother had a wonderful advantage being cared for by a teacher. I am sure she did homeschooling with Bill. Bill told me he was not unhappy with how he was raised. I think he stayed there because my grandparents had grown to love him, and my mother decided to let them raise him instead of taking him away when he went to kindergarten. The memories of our many good-byes still bring tears to my eyes.

My mom, my sister, and I would take the train to go see Bill. It would take a day to get there, and our visits always seemed so quick. Bill, Lois, and I would sob as we boarded the train to go back to Rochester. We never really understood why we had to be separated. Yet we accepted what we had to do. My heart still lays heavy from the memory of it. Bill had a picture hanging in his Belfast home of an angel with large wings encompassing two small children. Bill would point at them and call the angel our mom and Lois and me the children.

Pa's oldest son, William, took over the business when Pa retired. I know nothing about Uncle Bill except that he took over the meat market when Pa retired. Uncle Bill married Mary Effinger. For several years they helped raise Mary's niece and nephew, Loretta and John Effinger, after the children's parents died. They came every Sunday after ten o'clock Mass to visit Pa. They took two steps into the kitchen and stayed for only a half hour.

By that time Pa had some health problems. He had developed seizures due to a hardening of the arteries in his brain. Dr. Howard Burns came to see him after the first seizure. Dr. Burns said he was sorry to tell us, but the seizures would continue. These seizures most always occurred at night. Pa would moan or let out a scream and want to get out of bed. He was confused. His son-in-law, Uncle Joe, would gently encourage him to stay in bed. If he had one spell, which is what we called the seizures, there would usually be another and another. I was a young teenager, but the seizures frightened me. Pa was a big man. He wore one of the old-fashioned cutaway gowns. The look he had on his face as he stood in the hallway wearing that cutaway really scared me. I realize now that the look on his face was,

"What is happening to me? What am I doing?" There was probably some degree of fear for him as well. He would spend the next day in bed because the spell took such a toll on him. When he recovered his strength, he would say, "I had another spell didn't I?"

My maternal grandfather, Frank J. Vetter, died April 7, 1941, of prostate cancer and hardening of the arteries of the brain when he was seventy-seven years old. This man, of all men, deserved the most wonderful Mass for his burial. We could not have one for him because it was Good Friday. Good Friday is the day Jesus Christ was crucified; therefore, it is a day of reflection of what He did for us. We did celebrate a Mass for Pa at a later date, but without his body.

Pa was a gentle and caring man. He spoke very slowly and always listened attentively. He went to confession every Saturday. I questioned him once. I said, "Pa, you do nothing wrong, why do you go to confession every week?" He told me he went for the grace of the Sacrament.

There was a family meeting after Pa's death. William's wife wanted to be there as well. Pa didn't have much because of the market crash. His eldest daughter, Anna, asked if her husband, Joe, could have his watch. This thoughtful son-in-law sold his own home to help Pa out. He was there for Pa during all those seizures, and he took care of Anna's grand-mother and sister Huldy. Then, to top it all off, he and Anna welcomed my mother, sister, and me into their home. He certainly deserved the watch, but William's wife apparently didn't think so and stated as much. I hear there were some words, but Joe got the watch. I'm not sure what was said or even if the watch was of any monetary value. I think Aunt Anna wanted it for her husband for the kindness he had shown all of us.

SEVEN

BELFAST, NEW YORK

Gramma Healy and a visitor on the porch in Belfast, New York

My mother, sister, and I, along with our beautiful new-born brother, William Charles, left for Belfast, New York, just after his birth in April 19028. We stayed with him for a few weeks but left without him. My father's parents agreed to help out, and Bill ended up staying with them until he was eighteen years of age. It was his home. It's just that it was so far away from us. I was too young to remember at the time, but my mother later said she would never do it again. Somehow, she thought we would have gotten along. For a mother to leave her baby is heart wrenching. My mother's love was her strength. She knew Bill would be well cared for in his paternal grandparents' home. And they loved him very much. The love we had for each other was our strength. There was love for everyone and from everyone. There was never a lack of love for my sister, brother, and me.

Grampa Henry DeForest Healy Gramma Anna Fox Healy

I felt sorry to leave Bill in that small town. Today, at almost ninety, I would love to live there. Eighty miles was considered a very long distance in 1928. We did not own a car. Roads were rough. However, we could take the train, and we managed to visit a few times a year. When the old Erie Pennsylvania Railroad stopped running, we took a bus part of the way and then waited about two hours for a second bus to take us to Belfast. The trip took an entire day. Grampa Healy always met us at the train depot. There were only two people to a seat, but you could flip the back of one bench over and sit together facing each other. However, this meant someone had to ride facing backward. I always felt a little scared when we went over a high trestle with nothing on either side. Later some friends offered to drive us. My cousin Helen's husband, Al Grove, drove us a few times.

There was always sadness when we had to leave. The long trip back home without Bill just hurt, so there was very little to talk about. My brother would cry and cry when we'd leave. I know it was so painful for my mother. My own throat still gets a lump at the memory of leaving him. To this very day, a train whistle can provoke my emotions and can keep me from swallowing easily.

Despite these difficulties, we stayed extremely close. No siblings could be closer. Bill died on February 13, 2012. We never fought and always put love first.

Bill, June, and Lois Healy

There were special times when I would visit my brother and learn how he'd spend his days. In the early evening, we would take a milk pail and a lantern, since there weren't any streetlights, to get milk after it was strained. I will always remember the smell of Mrs. Houghton's kitchen, where she strained the milk. I think only someone who has smelled it could recognize the scent of strained milk. I'm not sure I know the words to describe it. Bill drank the unpasteurized milk because that is what they did that many years ago in small towns. Our mom did everything she could to avoid criticizing our grandmother, her mother-in-law. Mom didn't really approve of unpasteurized milk, but she let it be.

Gramma would let the milk set in the pail until all of the cream would float to the surface. She would use that thick cream to make a wonderful dessert topping for the many special pastries she often made. (I guess my sister, mother, and I did have the unpasteurized milk in the whipped cream!) Everyone who ate at Gramma's raved about her cooking. She was precise and the best at it. Gramma was the town baker, and Bill was her delivery boy. Her fried cakes were second to none, as we used to say.

I also recall that when Bill met our father in 1983, Bill enjoyed talking with him about growing up in Belfast. They had this experience in common, and it gave them something to talk about.

Bill participated in many high school activities, such as basketball, and he had many friends. We enjoyed visiting his school, the library, the little stores in town, and St. Patrick's Church. My grandmother was a Catholic but not as strong a believer as Mom about church. Gramma once said she wanted to take us to hear a beautiful choir in the Protestant church in Belfast. My mother said nothing to her about the Catholic teaching that salvation is only found in the Catholic Church and that Catholics should never go to Protestant churches. Or if they wanted to, they needed to get permission. Gramma was a Catholic too, but she obviously found nothing wrong with going to listen to the choir. After Vatican II in 1965, this teaching, of course, has completely changed. I'm not so sure how my mom got out of that one back in 1935.

Years ago, people liked to show you the new things they bought. We would all sit around while Gramma would bring out gifts she had received, still in their boxes. They could be nightgowns or petticoats, which are also known as slips. She would very carefully bring the boxes into the living room and ever so gently unwrap each box. Gramma would lift up the item from the box for everyone in the room to see.

There was a heat register on the floor that measured about thirty inches by thirty inches. Those heat vents were wonderful to stand on—just like Marilyn Monroe did, when her dress blew up from the air vent. We were told, of course, not to stand on the register. Bedroom doors were kept closed to keep the heat in the living area. In the evening Gramma would put hot stones in the beds to warm the sheets and covers. Very large, flat stones were put on the register to warm them up. Then we'd sink down in the warm feather beds and fall fast asleep. In the morning, we'd run to the heat blowing from that beautiful register in the morning chill.

Back then there was a chamber pot under the bed in case of an emergency in the night. The rim of the pot was always so cold.

On Christmas we went to bed around eight o'clock so we would stay awake at the midnight Mass. "O Holy Night" still brings me tears of joy and gives me a feeling of fullness in my heart. They always sang that hymn. The church was a lengthy walk in the bitter cold of New York without streetlights. I was always glad to go early to hear the choir prior to Mass.

Gramma would take us for a walk into town occasionally for an ice cream and a candy bar. Lois and I would wolf our candy bars down, but Bill would carefully eat his piece by piece. He would cut and eat a single piece, and then he would put the rest on the middle shelf of Gramma's cupboard. I remember checking on it regularly, and then I would run and tell Lois about Bill still not finishing his candy bar.

He was an only child in our grandparent's home in Belfast. Bill could have been very spoiled, but our grandmother was not the spoiling type.

When we would finish eating lunch, Gramma would say, "Would you like to walk down and see Mrs. Callahan?" The Callahans lived in a large lovely home with exceptionally beautiful glass doors. Of course, everyone, even the children, sat quietly at the Callahans' listening to many stories.

The house next door to Gramma's had five children. My grandmother would get very upset when those children were left alone. She always kept a close eye on the house.

Even after Bill left Belfast to live in Rochester, we still went back to Gramma's for clambakes. There was a playground across the street that Joe filmed. He would show the eight-millimeter film and run it backward to make us all laugh.

Gramma Anna was a strong, distinct, and disciplined woman. Her father, husband, and first son were a disappointment to her, but it never held her back from standing up for herself and giving my brother a warm, healthy, happy home. She loved him and taught him to be the man he was.

William Healy

EIGHT

MY MOTHER

My mother's retirement from Kodak.

There is no doubt in my mind about who most influenced the direction of my life and made me who I am: my mother. She was always truthful and honest. She never pretended something could be if it never could. Today people will tell you, "Go for it," "You can do it," and "Take chances." My mom had only kindness and consideration to and for others. Even with regard to our father, she would reassure us and say, "He is the one who lost out."

Mom did have the opportunity to date our dentist, Norman Levin. He asked her out many times. She never went because she was still legally married.

I call him our dentist, but for most of our grammar school years, we went to the dental dispensary where dental students worked on our teeth in their learning process. One morning a month, a teacher from Holy Redeemer School would take us downtown on the streetcar. I loved riding the streetcar, watching what we passed as we rode along. We each needed a nickel for the visit. It was a large building, and in the waiting room, there was a huge cage of tweeting birds. The singing of the birds was to help alleviate any fears. They did not help me; I still recall being afraid.

We would pay our nickel and get a number. When the number was called, someone would escort us into a room with approximately twenty men studying to be dentists. After they checked our teeth, if we needed any pulled, we went to another room. I do not recall it being a pleasant experience at all. In fact, remembering all those birds, I hear them now as a fair warning for pain to come.

Even so, I did enjoy school. We would arrive early, around 7:30 a.m. so we could go to eight o'clock Mass. At that time, in order to receive Holy Communion, you had to fast from eating from midnight the night before. Therefore, we only received Holy Communion on the first Friday of each month. It was hard to go that long without eating since our next meal would be lunch. So we'd get to bring our breakfast once a month to eat after Mass.

Receiving the Holy Eucharist was always special to me, but I will confess that I loved the breakfast Aunt Anna made for me after Mass. Aunt Anna would shop at Bond Bread Factory. She would purchase day-old bread and baked goods. I remember looking forward to the chocolate-covered cookie. Inside was a graham cracker with marshmallow filling and a half teaspoon of jelly in the middle of the marshmallow. So I guess I mean to say that I loved the desserts.

The Eucharist is a sacrament of the altar. It is a reminder of the Last Supper, in which Jesus gave His disciples bread and wine, saying they were His body and blood. The Catholic Church believes that when the bread and wine are consecrated in the Eucharist, they cease to be bread and wine and become the body and the blood of Christ. As a Catholic, I was taught to believe this even though the appearance and physical properties of the bread and wine are not changed. This was part of my faith from the day I was born.

We always went to the Bond Bread Factory to get day-old bread as well as some goodies. Aunt Anna would give us a list of what she needed. We would pull a cart quite a distance up North Street, which took us about a half hour each way. We would load the cart with several loaves of bread and some sweet goodies. I loved just standing in the bakery and smelling the wonderful aroma of the baking bread and pastries. Because the country was in the Depression, every bit of saving helped.

I was a pretty thin child. They called me "puny," so I was given a free glass of milk every day to help make me grow big and strong. After I had my tonsils out, I became healthier.

I loved Holy Redeemer School. I lived very close, so I had enough time to go home for lunch, which was sometimes toasted bread with a little sugar in warm milk. I still had time left over to get back to the playground for fun time. I remember me and my friends would run around after each other with much laughter and merriment. When the first bell would ring, we were taught to stop dead still wherever we were. Then the second bell meant we were to make a line to prepare to march into the school building. At the third bell, we would have to start marching to our classrooms.

Prayers were always said before class. Usually we'd recite the Hail Mary and Our Father. Sister always said the first part of each prayer, and we children responded with the second part of the prayer. Then we'd say the Pledge of Allegiance to the flag. I especially liked singing "Come, Holy Ghost." The song filled our hearts with hope and love, ultimately putting us in a thinking and receptive mood.

Come, Holy Ghost, Creator blest,
And in our hearts take up Thy rest;
Come with Thy grace and heav'nly aid
To fill the hearts which Thou hast made;
O Comforter, to Thee we cry,
Thou heav'nly gift of God most high;
Thou font of life and fire of love,
And sweet anointing from above;
Praise be to Thee, Father and Son,
And Holy Spirit, with them one;
And may the Son on us bestow
The gifts that from the Spirit flow.

My neighbor John Englert went through all eight years of school with me. He always used to credit me with helping him pass each year. When we were in the first grade, someone in the classroom whistled. The teacher asked who had whistled. No one claimed to have done it, so all of the boys had to stay after school. Girls never whistled, so it had to be one of the boys. I went up to the teacher and told her that John didn't know how to whistle, so he really needn't be punished. I'm not sure if my valiant efforts for him did any good.

My mom provided all of the opportunities for me. She loved her children and family with her whole heart and soul. She lived a life of example by the ways she always gave and received. I'm lucky to have had her for my mom, for the love that she gave and the example she set.

My grammar school graduation

NINE

CHURCH, HIGH SCHOOL, WORK, AND WAR

Our home at 987 was our nucleus, but we spent a lot of time doing church activities as well. There was a lot of community life back then. We had roller-skating, bingo, basketball, festivals, picnics, drama club, and many church devotions. May devotions were to honor and show our love for Jesus's mother. Sacred Heart devotions took place in June. During Forty Hours devotions, the Blessed Sacrament was exposed for forty hours. Each class spent time in meditation. Then there were the Stations of the Cross, where we could follow Christ's journey to Calvary, noting the sorrows He undertook for our salvation.

Lenten services helped us realize that it is good to sacrifice for the good of others. As I learned over the years, sacrificing for others is also good for ourselves. Advent services helped prepare us for the celebration of the birth of Christ.

There were tea dances on Sunday afternoons in the school hall. I knew many of the boys who played in the band from Aquinas High School. I watched the basketball games and belonged to the drama club. I belonged to the Sodality as well as the Youth Group. I even took bit parts in plays. The one in particular that I enjoyed was the Passion play. I just had to sit there in a garden-type setting, pretending to embroider. It was such fun just being with my friends. We were always laughing.

A lucky event in my life was when I was sitting in the library doing reference work. The head librarian, Vera Cooke, asked me if I would consider a part-time job in the library. I would have never guessed I would work at the library for forty-four years.

I started as a page at Portland Library in 1941. A page files books and does what is called reading the shelves to ensure proper order. I would run down Lake Avenue to catch the cross-town bus; if you missed one, it was a twenty-minute wait for the next. I usually worked from 3:00 to 6:00 p.m., but sometimes my boss, Miss Cooke, would ask me to work until 9:00 p.m. I would occasionally take a short break in the back room during the longer hours. When the children came in from school around 3:30 p.m., they pulled out books and made havoc of the place. I would have to reshelve those books.

I checked books out to patrons as well. There weren't any computers, so we wrote out everything in longhand. Each book had a slip. Depending on what color it was, it was put into a slot. The Dewey decimal system used colors to identify different sections. Matching up the returned books with their colors made shelving easier.

Occasionally, I had to help out at library's Lincoln Branch, which was on the corner of Joseph Avenue and Clifford Avenue. The two large blocks that I had to walk home could be scary when I worked till 9:00 p.m. In the darkness, I had to walk past Washington Junior High, a long block without lights. When I walked by houses with lights on inside, I felt comforted.

December 7, 1941, Pearl Harbor Day, changed our lives. My three cousins, along with many friends, went off to war. I remember many times at Central Railroad Station saying good-bye to my drafted friends and hearing that dreaded train whistle. I wrote many letters and listened to many radio forecasts. Gabriel Heater was the forecaster for those reports. My aunt Anna listened attentively to what he said, since her three sons were drafted. He would usually start with, "There is good news tonight." We knew not to speak during the forecast. My aunt Anna aged in those years. I think her eye twitching started then and continued for many years. Her son Ray went to the Pacific theater with the navy, Joe went to the European theater, and Bob stayed in America in the air force.

Joe Placious

Ray Placious   Bob Placious

We stood in line for butter, counted ration coupons, and prayed for the war to end. We had air raid practices where everything was turned off and we sat very still in the darkness and silence. I always had an eerie feeling during those times. A siren would sound for the start of the practice air raid and then again when it was over. This was to prepare us for any type of invasion. Many people suffered because of war in France, Germany, Italy, Japan, and the Ukraine. America was preparing for any event. We would get directions from the radio. No one, except the air raid wardens, was on the street. We really had no idea how bad it was.

In retrospect, that war stands out in the history of genocides as the most horrifying. We lost two neighbors in the war, Nunzio Mancuso and Walter Kiefer. My cousins all returned OK. Ray was stung by a Portuguese man-of-war and suffered from that. The sting from this marine cnidarian is not like that of a common jellyfish in that the cnidarian's venomous tentacles produce a very painful sting.

John Knobel, Lois's boyfriend, was in the European theater. Lois, my best friend, Julia, and I visited John in Detroit, Michigan, when he was in the service. John got a couple of cute sailors for Julia and me, and we all went out dancing for the evening.

TEN

STANLEY

I met a boy in 1941 when I was about sixteen. His name was Stanley Ciecierski. Because of his high blood pressure, the military classified him 4F, or unfit for service. He went to Edison Tech High School with my cousins Ray and Bob. Stanley came to our home often. When we started dating, he would take me to the movies or downtown to live shows, which we both enjoyed. Date nights years ago were Tuesday, Thursday, Saturday, and Sunday. Sometimes we would double date—with Lois and John or Ray and Julia. We often went to the Holy Redeemer Athletic Association Club where you could bowl, play cards, and use the slot machines. We'd usually end up going to the amusement park called Sea Breeze. Then we'd go over to our favorite hamburger joint, Harry's Hots Restaurant. Stanley gave me a very beautiful necklace with cubic zirconium stones on it one Christmas. Then on Christmas day in 1943, looking forward to marriage, he gave me a wonderful cedar chest.

On our usual Thursday night date, Stanley didn't come over. The next day I went to his home to find out that he was hospitalized in Rochester General Hospital. That night after work I took the bus to the hospital to visit him. He seemed OK to me; he was in good spirits and happy to see me. The next morning when I called the hospital to talk with him, the person who answered asked me who I was. I told her that I was his girlfriend. She told me to call his family because he died that morning.

Catherine McIntyre, my boss at the library at that time, was extremely kind to me after I hung up the phone and told her what I had heard. Catherine called a taxicab to take me home.

Stanley died on February 9, 1944. He had just turned twenty-one the month before. He was laid out in an open casket with black patent leather shoes. He had a sister who was fourteen years older than he was and a brother twelve years older. Stanley was a prized brother to them. There was great sadness.

It was a heartbreaking time for me. My mom's heart was broken for me. I was eighteen years old. While I was worrying about my family fighting World War II, my boyfriend died at home of uremic poisoning.

Eleven

Getting Married

Elwood and I on a date

I eventually joined the church's bowling team where, five months later, I met the man I would marry. He was a widower with a twelve-year-old daughter named Janice. My mom told me he had many strikes against him: he was fourteen years older than I was, not a Catholic, had been married with a child, and had a bone disease called osteomyelitis. I could see or hear none of this. I was smitten. I had fallen deeply and sincerely in love with him. He was kind, generous, fun loving, caring, sincere, and honest in addition to being handsome and daring. And I could see that he loved his daughter.

He was a good father. That was important to me. I told him I could not marry him if he did not intend to have more children. Mom eventually grew to love him too.

The first time Elwood came over to meet my mother, I told him to ignore everyone else who would be sitting on the front porch. Remember, there were eleven people living in this house, and they were all pretty strong personalities. Elwood, wearing a suit and tie, came in and met my mother. He looked so handsome. When we left, we said good-bye to everyone. After we drove away and Elwood turned the corner, he pulled the car over. He got out of the car and took his jacket and tie off. When he got back in the driver's seat behind the wheel, he looked at me and breathed a big sigh of relief. He was sure glad that moment was over; he so wanted my mother to like him. We courted, and he took some ribbing because of our age difference.

We married sixteen months later on November 17, 1945. Mr. and Mrs. Elwood George Heidt. Unfortunately, because of church regulations, we could not have a Mass, just the ceremony.

Our Wedding day

We were allowed to walk down the aisle, but not enter the sanctuary. I had a Mass said the morning of our wedding day at 7:00 a.m. I asked for God's blessing on our marriage. We were married at 9:00 a.m. in the church. Prior to being allowed to marry in a Catholic church, the marriage between a Catholic and a non-Catholic was considered a mixed marriage and the ceremony would be performed in the rectory. The church is a living church and continues to make wonderful changes as time moves forward. Granted, it is slow moving, but what a tremendous responsibility leaders have to guide their flock to their final destination.

My mom gave me a lovely dinner at Rose Carlin's restaurant with a reception in our home. I have some regrets about not wearing a wedding gown and veil, but my mom discouraged me. She said it was because we were not being married with a Mass, with only a fifteen-minute ceremony. Spending the money for a wedding gown and veil might have been too costly. I did look lovely, which my new husband told me many times. I wore a pale yellow suit with brown accessories.

June, Elwood, and Janice Heidt

We left by train for a week's stay in New York City for our honeymoon. Even though my husband was fourteen years older than I, he had not traveled much. He had been orphaned at seventeen. Therefore, he was thrilled with everything: the train ride, the buildings, the crowds of people in the city. I remember waking up in the middle of the night to find him looking out the window, amazed at the activity at such a late hour.

When we returned home, I started keeping house and caring for Janice. Elwood went back to work. I planned my meals down to the last detail. I often called my aunt Anna for pointers. Everything was new; I had never washed, cooked, ironed, or tended a fire. There was a coal furnace in our home. Coal was sent down a shoot into the basement. The furnace needed coal added regularly. My husband was very patient with me. He would explain in great detail how the furnace worked in a loving and caring way.

He was always trying to make life better, easier, and nicer. He built shelves in our living room, changed the entire kitchen around, and put a shower in the bathroom. Our basement was only under the living room and bedroom section of the house, so Elwood started digging and digging. He would bring the dirt up and carry it away. He bought a little box trailer and so many times filled it with dirt. Eventually, we had a full basement under the entire house. My husband spent lots of time at his workbench in that basement. I used to call down to him, "How long are you going to be down there?" or "When are you coming back up?" He would say, "Put a jacket on and come on down."

There was a trap door in our kitchen to the basement. Elwood made an outside and an inside entrance to the full basement. Both entrances had stairwells with railings. He never seemed to tire of finding projects.

11 Borchard Street, before and after we
had the front porch enclosed.

I remember once I awoke in the middle of the night to find Elwood standing with his back to the wall. I couldn't really see what he was doing. I called out "Elwood" as loudly and sharply as I could. He jumped and asked me what was wrong. He was clearly surprised to hear me yell out his name. I explained that I wasn't sure what he was doing and thought perhaps he was sleepwalking. He said he was scratching his back on the edge of the doorframe. I went back to sleep and thought, "He gets a back scratcher for Christmas."

TWELVE

OUR CHILDREN

When I found myself pregnant, we were delighted and immediately started preparing.

Pregnant with Edward

We wanted a son, but we were prepared for God's will. My husband's father's name was Edward. I loved my husband so much, so in trying to please him, I suggested naming our first child Edward if it was a boy. We were all delighted to welcome Edward into our family. Elwood was very attentive to Eddie, and he lovingly carried him around our home telling him all about the house. Janice also loved her brother, and she had many friends who took an interest in him. Eddie was about one year old when we learned we were pregnant again.

Pregnant with James

This time we just prayed for a healthy baby, but as we talked we thought of how they would only be twenty months apart and that another son would be special. We discussed the first name for what might be a second son, such as Larry or Tom, but I knew El liked James.

Baby Jim surprised us. We were expecting him on July 20, but our little firecracker was born on the Fourth of July. Jim's obstetrician said, "You have a little firecracker with a fuse."

Eddie and Jimmy were both born on Sundays—Eddie at 4:45 a.m. and Jimmy at 4:45 p.m. I suggested using Elwood for his middle name. Again, my way of showing my great love for my husband. Everyone welcomed Jimmy and was very happy for us.

I was as happy as I could imagine with my family. Janice was a wonderful daughter who helped me out many times with her brothers. El was thrilled with his daughter and now two sons.

Jimmy did some crying and was fussy before bedtime. Big brother Eddie would try to help calm Jimmy by tossing all of their toys in the crib on top of him. My husband suggested putting him on his stomach. The sheet was taut and there wasn't anything else in the crib to cause problems, so I tried it. Jimmy loved it, falling fast asleep. Today, parents make sure their children sleep on their backs for safety because of possible infant crib death.

Janice and I got along well. I went to parents' happenings at Nazareth High School. She got a job at the library, and I would pick her up when she finished her shift. She readily babysat for us. Janice and her friends brought much laughter and fun into our home.

Janice stayed with us until her marriage at twenty-three years of age. She married Dick Townsend, a childhood friend, in Our Lady of Perpetual Help church on May 12, 1956. Dick studied the Catholic faith and was baptized prior to their marriage. I was his godmother. They found an apartment near us on Farbridge Street, about four blocks away. Then, a year later, one evening after dinner, they announced that they had decided to move to California. Dick was an Otis elevator repairman; Janice was a secretary. They knew they could find work anywhere. They were young with lots of hopes and dreams like we had been. Soon they were settled in California. They eventually found work as sales reps as they were both friendly and charismatic. They did very well for many years. They had two children, a son and daughter. Today their children are both married with children of their own. Life moves faster than you can possibly realize.

When Edward was seven and James was five, I became pregnant again. We really prayed for a daughter, but always respected God's will. Our daughter was born during a heavy snowstorm on March 30, 1954. She was a lovely spring awakening. Of course, little did I know that the snowstorm may have been fair warning for her teenage years. She was just a sweet little baby girl when she was born. She was so easy to care for, and I was a bit older. Janice was a young adult at this point, and our sons were in school. So my time was a bit freer to enjoy Ruthanne. Janice took a week's vacation from her full-time job at Westinghouse Corporation as a secretary, to help with her brothers.

Elwood's sister, Ruth, and her husband, Bob, lived upstairs. Elwood and Ruth were left the house when their mom died. They both quit school and started working to pay for the house. It was a duplex, so Ruth moved upstairs and Elwood lived downstairs. Ruth and Bob had a son, but Ruth loved our children, her nieces and nephews. Ruth was also a big help. Aunt Ruth could not be a godmother, so we decided on naming our daughter Ruthanne after Aunt Ruth, as an honor to her. I thought Ruth and Anne went well together. My aunt Anna, who raised me while my mom worked, was very dear to me, as was my grandmother, Anna Healy. I came up with Ruthanne's name to honor those special women. Ruth was also mentioned in the Bible as having strength of character. When she was sixteen, Ruthanne became a page at Hudson Library, just like I did at sixteen.

Janice and I

Jimmy, Edward, Ruthanne, Elwood and I

Our family, including our extended family, was our life. We played and vacationed together. We visited relatives who also had young children. My cousins had children of their own: Helen had two daughters, Joe had a son and daughter, Ray had five children, and Bob had five children. Lois had four daughters, and my brother Bill had three girls and two boys. We would meet regularly at 987 on Sunday afternoons to sing, play games and cards, and eat buns and cupcakes from Quality Bakery dunked in coffee. El took the children to the zoo, ice-skating, boating, and sleigh riding. He put up sandboxes, swings, a swimming pool, a skating rink, horse-shoes, and a basketball net in the driveway. Dad was inter-ested in everything. He loved to learn, teach, and give. I recall our neighbor, John Rossner, would put water on his driveway during the winter creating a large ice-skating rink for the neighborhood. Dad would sharpen skates for the children. We lived in a wonderful neighborhood where everyone knew each other. We'd all sit out some nights after dinner and actually chat back and forth from our porches!

Elwood was a den father for the boys' Cub Scout troop. He prepared many projects for them. We'd help with selling jellybeans for the scouts too. Those were the happiest years of my life. I found pleasure in keeping house, preparing meals, being a wife and parent. I would anxiously await the arrival of my family after their day in their world. My early years were good, and my twilight years are OK, but if I had any years to live over again, they would be my married years.

My husband drank more than he should have sometimes. He also had a quick temper. But for me, all this was balanced by his kindness and caring nature all of the other times. Overall, the good far outweighed the bad.

Our life went on with the usual births, baptisms, confirmations, graduations, weddings, and deaths. Our gatherings and annual vacations as a large, loving family were celebrated with fun, laughter, and tears.

We had so much to be thankful for. We communicated easily about our hopes and dreams, for ourselves as well as our children. I believe Dad was a Catholic by desire. He would so many times tell me over and over again that he wished he could believe and practice as I did.

THIRTEEN

FAMILY VACATIONS

Ray Placious, Elwood Heidt, June Healy,
Julia Taylor, John Knobel, Bill Healy

E very year from about 1950 through 1970, our family vacationed in the Adirondack Mountains. We stayed at a place called Eagle Bay at Fourth Lake in what is known as the Fulton Chain of Lakes. The entire family would caravan to Eagle Bay every summer. Our car would lead the way because Elwood towed his boat. John and Lois and their four girls followed, then Bill and Lorraine and their five children, then Ray and Julia and their five children. Bob and Terry and their five children would join, as would Joe and Millie and their two children. Helen and Al and their two girls also stayed at one of the small cottages. They often shared cottages with Uncle Ray or Uncle Bob's families. Everyone joined together to eat meals, to relax at the beach, and to play euchre in the evening. We were inseparable.

John and Lois and their girls would share a cabin with my family. Bill and Lorraine would stay at the polka dot cabin, a stone's throw away. Ray and Julia also stayed nearby. We would bring everything with us: food, drinks, beach toys, cards, etc. As soon as we arrived, we would clean the cabin and then unload our things. The children liked to pick out their rooms. There were two master suites for John and Lois and Elwood and me.

The kids were always anxious to get right down to the beach. In the early years, they had to wait for us because they were too young to go by themselves. In the later years, we'd let them go ahead of us. We would all take sandwiches and snacks with us for lunch, along with lots of beverages. We'd spend our days at the beach. Then we would go back to the cabin to make dinner and relax and visit. We enjoyed playing euchre before we went off to bed. Euchre is a card game that our family played for many years. We'd sing all evening long. We all loved to sing. It was a week of being together, filled with laughter and joy.

We'd go to the local ice cream store, the shops in the little town of Inlet, and then The Trading Post. The kids loved the Trading Post because it had so many stuffed wild animals on the walls. Above them hung the heads of deer, buffalo, and various other wild animals that had been caught.

The older kids would see movies and go horseback riding, but the day's main event was the beach. We'd go swimming, boating, and water skiing. There were a couple of years where it rained pretty much the whole time we were there. Those vacations were tough with so many kids, but we found ways to have fun regardless.

So we'd spend seven glorious days a year at Eagle Bay. Minus two days for cleaning. Everyone pitched in to clean when we got there, and then we'd clean up our own mess when we left. I often wonder if everyone did that. I guess it seems silly to clean the cabin after someone else and then clean it up for the next family who would rent it.

Then there were our miniature vacations. These we would generally take with my sister and her family. Elwood and John became very good friends. In fact, sometimes Lois and I would wonder where they were together. They often got lost going to some fishing store when they went out to shop. Eventually, they'd come home, but not before a stop off at the local bar. We had a bar at the corner of our street named Otto's. We spent a lot of time in that place. Sometimes the kids would be with us. There were various games for them to play while we visited in the bar. We also liked to go to Niagara Falls on the weekend. We found a place with an indoor pool, so sometimes we'd go in the winter as well.

I remember one year we decided spontaneously to spend a Fourth of July weekend in Niagara Falls. We headed out early in the morning. The kids kept asking us to find a place with a pool. We drove to I don't remember how many places, but there were no vacancies. How naïve of us to think we could just go there on the Fourth of July and get rooms. I remember Ruthanne waking up in the back seat of the car asking if we were there yet; I turned to her and quietly said, "No, we're home. It's midnight. Go to bed." And that was the end of that.

There were so many years of parties at our house. In the summertime, after we purchased an above-ground pool, we invited everyone to come over to swim and keep cool in the summer. They were pleasurable days of fun.

Once a month we'd meet for games of euchre. We each took a turn as host. We would sing and laugh; it was the time of my life. Although sometimes my husband would have one too many drinks. We'd be driving home and he would pull over to sing a song to me. I knew he loved me, as it was generally a love song such as "If I had My Life to Live Over" or "Let Me Call You Sweetheart." But I was not feeling my drinks as he was, so I felt ready to go to bed. However, sometimes those are the times I think I miss the most. The best memories are of his love for me.

I will say that often I was not happy when Elwood drank too much. I never saw him as irresponsible, but having a beer was important to him. He enjoyed it more than I did. He always enjoyed a smoke and a beer. It was one of our few differences. Regardless of the ups and downs of marriage, though, I never felt distanced from my husband. We could always talk. We always laughed. And, yes, a fight now and then. The older I get the more I realize there were more good times than bad. And I am grateful.

FOURTEEN

SAYING GOOD-BYE AND MOVING FORWARD

Jimmy, Edward and Ruthanne meet Santa

E dward was the next of our children to leave after Janice. In 1965, he told us he wanted to be a teaching priest in the Basilian order. We, along with many of our extended family, caravanned in our car to Pontiac, Michigan, where Ed moved to start his religious life. Many miles passed during our drive home before I could swallow. He was nineteen years old. My oldest boy was becoming a man. I am sure all people have felt that lump in their throat at some time or another. Both Janice and Edward were following their own dreams, which was what we taught them to do, so how could we really be sad for long. They were heading out in their own direction. The postman would bring welcome news of their affairs and activities. We knew from their letters that they were happy.

Janice, James, and Ruthanne all left home at the age of twenty-three. Ed left just before his nineteenth birthday. Jim met his future wife, Carmella, a few months before Dad died in June 1970. I have always been pleased that Dad met Carm, even though marriage was not mentioned at the time. Carm brought a lot of happiness into our family. She fit right in and enjoyed being with Jim, which made me happy too. My children's happiness has often been my happiness. Jim and Carm had a lovely wedding in October 1971. Within two years, they bought a beautiful house. Their first child, Danielle, like her dad, entered our beautiful world on a Sunday. I really felt my cup overflowing. Their second daughter, Jessica, followed, and then came their son, Matthew. Their children are three positively lovely, unique, charming personalities. Jim and Carm loved to play racquetball, go to the movies, or visit friends' homes, and I loved to babysit for them.

Ruthanne had visited her sister, Jan, in California when she was fourteen years old. As a young adult, she decided she would follow her sister's lead and make California her home too. I helped Ruthanne with all of her plans. I drove across the country with her to help set her up in her new home. I stayed until she was settled with a job. We found a nice apartment for her, and then I flew home alone. I felt like a traitor and betrayer to myself. My little girl was so far away. I missed her. When I look back on it all now, I do not know how I ever had the strength to leave her so alone, so many miles from home, from me. She has done well. She got a very responsible job that she enjoyed. She met the man she would one day marry, George. Ruthanne became a stepmother to George's daughter, Jessica. They had many happy times traveling, camping, and fishing. Ruthanne never had any children other than Jessica, whom she truly loves. Ruthanne felt that she was a caring, loving adult in Jessica's life.

Edward, Janice, Ruthanne and Jim

The great happiness I had growing up with all of my family living so close was not to be for my children. My two daughters chose to live many, many miles away, as did my eldest son. We are still close, with videos, phone calls, and now Skype, and we still have vacations where we see each other. I really feel their love, but I miss their presence. My children have always been and always will be my joy.

FIFTEEN

MY HUSBAND

A lthough this was not a happy moment, I have to tell you about it.

My husband suffered a heart attack early in life. He was fifty-two. It was 1963. The attack did not damage his heart too severely, but seven years later, he suffered a fatal one. On June 28, 1970, I lost the most important and loving man I've ever known. I was crushed. He would have been fifty-nine on his next birthday. We were planning to renew our vows in November. We would have been married twenty-five years. My heart breaks just from the memory of such a painful loss. I felt my future was in distress. I had just turned forty-five years old on June 3. I still had to raise our sixteen-year-old daughter. How could I live without this wonderful man?

It was in the middle of the night. He woke up with great discomfort, so I called an ambulance. He paced back and forth and kept saying, "When is this pain going to stop." I never felt so helpless.

I remember that I felt great relief when the ambulance arrived. I saw them put an oxygen mask for breathing on his face. I thought everything would be all right then. When I rode in the ambulance, the man in the back with Dad made a joking remark to make sure everyone was awake at the hospital. I remember laughing about this. I hadn't a clue of how serious this really was. I never even imagined I might lose my husband. Just before I got into the ambulance, my husband's sister, Ruth, called from the upstairs window. She wanted to know what was wrong. I called up to her as quietly as I could, so as not to upset my husband that I thought he might be having another heart attack. After the ambulance left, my son Jim came home from a party and went to bed. Our house was locked, so Ruth went downstairs and knocked on the outside of his bedroom window to wake him and tell him what had happened.

Jim came to the hospital. I will be forever grateful that he was there with me. My daughter, Ruthanne, was sleeping over at a friend's house, so she didn't experience any of this. Jim and I waited. We could see them working on Dad. Someone finally shut the door so we could no longer see. When they came out, they told us he was DOA, dead on arrival. He died in the ambulance. That man in the back of the ambulance was worried when he made what I thought was a joke. They were trying to bring him back when we were watching them. They suggested we not see Dad's body at that time. Shock is pretty much the only word for what I felt at this dreadful news. Shock. Disbelief. Somehow I got through the most horrible moment in my life. Somehow.

I found leaving him at the cemetery the hardest part. I would never see him again. I know that the soul is gone; the body no longer feels any pain. But I grieved at how alone I felt without him in the wee hours of the night. How would I ever laugh again? I had no choice but to survive.

Elwood's life was not the easiest. In 1917, his own dad died of pneumonia at twenty-eight. El was only six years old. His mother died in 1929 at the age of forty-two. My husband was almost eighteen and his sister was sixteen. Their mother had just bought their home in 1925. Their stepfather took everything he could from the house and left. They didn't have any family to help them. They both quit Washington Junior High School and looked for full-time jobs. They then went to the bank and told them their story. The bank said to just pay the interest on the house for now, which enabled them to keep their home. Ruth got a job at the flower shop. Elwood set up pins at a bowling alley. He also did whatever odd jobs he could. He was very handy and could pretty much figure out anything. He wasn't afraid to ask and learn. Finally, he got a full-time job at Curl Lash. Curl Lash was a company downtown on South Avenue, right across from the library. They manufactured eyelash curlers. He had worked there for many years when finally a friend of his, Eddie Florack, asked if he would like to stack sheets at Great Lakes Press, where Eddie worked. Lithography became Elwood's specialty. I don't believe anyone worked harder than my husband, and, yes, I am probably biased. His hard work and interest in learning made him successful. He was so grateful for finding a good job. He and Eddie remained lifetime friends.

He loved all he could do, even with what we referred to as his "bum leg." The osteomyelitis caused his right leg to be shorter than the left. He also could not bend at the hip. We always had to help him put his sock on his right foot. I remember he created a shoehorn on the end of a folded yardstick so he could reach his ankle without bending. I have often thought he should have patented and marketed that invention. When the children were old enough to help him, he would ask, "Can somebody sock me?" He had such a wonderful sense of humor.

This photo was taken at Christmastime in 1969 and developed in November 1970—four months after Elwood's death.

When Elwood was about ten years old, he went to the firehouse just at end of Driving Park Bridge where there was a big hill. Going down the hill on his sled, he scraped his leg pretty badly. He did not tell his mom until it became infected. It had gone to the bone and he had osteomyelitis. He lost a year of school due to several scrapings of the bone. They just pulled the skin together without stiches because they knew they would have to scrape the bone often. He met several people with osteomyelitis. They had it break out in many parts of their body. His devoted mom did everything and tried everything suggested. I remember Elwood telling me that she once took the membrane out of an egg and put in on his leg.

Elwood spent a lot of his childhood in hospitals. But he held on to hope. He had a mother who loved him. While bedridden, he learned to sew and do things with his hands. The doctors wanted to remove his leg. It wasn't healing. His mother said no. She would do everything she could to help heal that large gash that went from his knee to his hip on the outside of his right thigh.

Penicillin wasn't introduced into society until Elwood was thirty-three years old. During wartime, penicillin was saved for our fighting men. In 1944, he went into the hospital and had round-the-clock injections of penicillin every four hours for three weeks. In case he had a flare-up, they taught him how to inject himself at home. A flare-up consisted of pain and oozing but no blood. It required boiling the needle, which I gladly did, before injecting the penicillin wherever there was a good muscle, such as arms, his left thigh, and, of course, his buttocks. His sister, Ruth, gladly helped her brother as well. My brother Bill was dating a nurse during that time. When she and Bill were visiting us, Elwood asked if she would like to give him his shot, and she did. Usually the pain made him realize he needed the penicillin. Eventually, the flare-ups stopped. Thank God for Dr. Alexander Fleming, who discovered penicillin.[2]

On her deathbed, his mother told Elwood not to marry. She said he would be a burden to a wife. Instead, he married twice. He loved and respected his mother deeply. She was right about many things, but not this. He was the best husband and father anyone could wish for. He loved and gave himself to me and his children.

There were very few, if any, people who did not like Elwood. I think the happiness of his accomplishments, against all odds, were his crowning glory.

We would talk often into the night of how wonderful our lives were. We were able to offer our children things we never had: education, dance classes, ice-skating opportunities, and summer vacations at the beach with waterskiing, horseback riding, and going to the movies. Our children got to be children. They didn't need to worry about where they would live or how the bills would be paid. We gave them a safe home with three meals a day. We offered our children every type of opportunity to learn and become good citizens.

---

2 http://www.pbs.org/newshour/rundown/the-real-story-behind-the-worlds-first-antibiotic/

Our sons and his daughter were adults when he died, but our youngest daughter was sixteen. The sixties and seventies were not easy years to raise a child alone, and Ruthanne was no picnic. She challenged everything that came her way. I loved her deeply but always feared for her. She and I rarely saw eye to eye in her teenage years. But we survived, and that is something. My nature is not to seek help or divulge my innermost fears or anxieties. My faith was my stronghold. I prayed constantly for the safety of my children. Their lives were mine. I wanted to be there for them whenever they needed me. They were my total enjoyment. I chose to be this way. They were busy and active, which pleased me. I never did care for cocktail parties or superficial conversation. I most enjoyed being with my children and their friends.

I worked, swam, took dance lessons, walked, read, did housework, cooked, watched television, went to the movies, and attended many church services. I always worship alone. Sometimes life seems so simple.

I would have loved to have had more years with Elwood. What a joy it would be to have my family there too. I miss not having been at my daughter's wedding. With Ed being a priest, he spends most of his time away from Rochester. I know there is much to feel good about: I was happily married with a lovely family, shared lots of laughter, and remained close to my entire family of siblings and cousins. But I have a special closeness to God. Only God's help could have gotten me through it all. I do believe God counts the hairs on your head and knows you by name.

SIXTEEN

MY GOLDEN YEARS AND REFLECTION

There are many experiences or occasions I have not talked about, experiences that were bummers for me. I hurt and ache, and sometimes my heart feels just like it does when I hear that dreadful train whistle. I feel scared, lost, and incomplete. My consolation is that God knows what is happening. I trust Him. I trust His love for me. I'll never cease asking Him to watch over and guard my family. When something gets too big for me, I turn it over to God. He has never let me down.

These golden years have been the toughest. I see our country changing. I see violence, unemployment, recession, and people leaving God out of everything. I am sure each generation saw change. My generation saw the development of cars, airplanes, radios, and TV. We don't have to defrost refrigerators anymore. We have automatic furnaces, hot water always on tap, expressways, and much better roads. Elwood was particularly fascinated to watch new expressways be constructed. He would go down on Sundays and see how far they got each week by actually driving on the road.

I was about twelve when we got our first refrigerator. Children were not allowed to open the refrigerator. Before we got it, we had an icebox. The iceman delivered 25, 30 and 40 pound chunks of ice. We would put a sign in our window to show what size we wanted. Kids liked to steal the chips of ice from the bed of the truck while the iceman was delivering ice. Lois got caught once and ran home quickly with the iceman running after her. He just wanted to see if she was OK because she jumped so quickly off the truck when he came back.

There were times when we were having supper when we would hear a plane. We would all run out to look up at it flying above our home. I was twelve or thirteen when we got our first phone. It was called a party line. Ours was a four-party line. If wc picked the phone up and someone was on it, we had to hang up immediately. We were told to wait several minutes before picking up the phone again to see if the line was free. When we made a call, we spoke to the operator. The operator would place the call for us. Our number was Stone 1094R. Gramma Healy in Belfast had a phone with a crank on the side of the phone. She would turn the crank to get the operator and ask, "Clara, get me Fran" and Clara would make the connection.

I have elderly friends who are sick, and their families are miles away. With all of the time-saving devices of today, I have never seen people busier. There doesn't seem to be any time to sit on the porch or have a chat over the back fence.

One of the worst changes is that children have to be bussed or chauffeured everywhere. I remember the fun of walking home from school with a pal. In the winter, with the snow piled high, we would climb up and walk over the shoveled mounds. We walked downtown. We walked to the ice-skating rink. It was a pretty long walk, but we enjoyed talking about skating and anticipating the fun we would have. Of course, when we were finished, we had to change back into our shoes in those cold and damp wood houses. The long trudge home wasn't as fun as going there. But there was hot cocoa and a snack waiting when we got home, which was nice.

I often wonder how my mother's feelings affected the baby in her womb as well as her two and four-year-old daughters. Should she have stayed put, not moved into her sister's home, and just done her best on her own? What could she have done without money? Many wealthy people hate giving what they have worked so hard for to anyone else. There wasn't any help from the government at that time. There was no social security or welfare program—what some called giveaway programs. I know some people work the system, but there are genuine requests for aid when life throws a curveball at you. When we needed a little help, our pastor took us to the shoe store at Christmas time to buy my sister and me new shoes and galoshes. At that time, the church took up a diocesan needs collection. That collection helped my mother, sister, and me.

My paternal grandparents loved us. They did what they could to help. I remember little of their parents. I do remember my great-grandfather Eugene Healy, who lived a very long life. But my memory consists of visiting him when he was bedridden and quite old.

My paternal grandfather, Henry DeForest Healy, fathered a child at the age of sixteen. The girl's parents kept the child in their home, using their last name for the child. We never did meet her. HD, as he was called, or sometimes "Cap," did fun things when Lois and I would visit at ages three and five years old. I especially remember him with a rabbit pull toy that was on wheels. He would somehow sneak an egg under the rabbit as he pulled the toy. He would sit by the heat register with a large board across his knees and play solitaire. He chewed tobacco. It constantly ran down the corners of his mouth.

As I said earlier, my grandfather was a drinker, but he stopped drinking in his early sixties when he retired. He had worked as a telephone man. He would repair phone lines by climbing the tall phone poles to repair the wires. Sometimes he would go into people's homes to install a phone for them. My grandmother's father, Billie Fox, was a heavy drinker too. He actually saw demons on the wall. I guess they were called the delirium tremens (dt's). Billie's wife, Maggie Berrigan Fox, was strong like my grandmother Anna Fox Healy, her daughter. I am unsure what the problem was with Grandfather Fox's burial after he died. Maggie just said, "He will be buried by the church and in this cemetery." And he was.

Should my mother have left my brother with our grandparents in Belfast? We were denied what we thought was a normal life, but for us, in retrospect, our life was good. My aunt and her family had also been denied what would have been a normal life with only one family in one home. My grandparents were fifty-two years old when they took Billy. My mother felt there was no other way. She was fortunate enough to have strong family support during what must have been a tremendously sad time for her.

Lois, Bill, and June

June, Bill, and Lois

My mother went to Holy Redeemer School through the sixth grade. She finished grades seven and eight at Nazareth Academy. From there, she went to work for Kodak. Mom resigned when she married. When my father left and Mom got us all settled at 987, she returned to Kodak, finishing out her working years there. When she returned to Kodak, they asked her who would be taking care of her children. Since Mom was responsible, she had no problem explaining her situation. Today they would not be allowed to ask such a personal question. Mom walked several large blocks from Hudson and Clifford Avenues to State and Brown Streets to the Kodak offices, saving the nickel the streetcar would have cost. When she was a little older, she started taking the bus, and I would meet her when she got off.

Mom left for work before I was awake in the morning, returning about five o'clock. Then she would help around the house. I know she did all of the ironing. I realize now in retrospect, at 90 years of age, that my father's decision to leave us not only affected us (my mom, my sister and brother and myself) but also affected our larger, extended family. The wisdom I gained from this experience is that human beings are all connected; no one person acts in isolation from others. Personal actions and decisions affect more than just the individual who makes them. Lois recalled to me one time when Pa overheard Aunt Anna complaining to a neighbor about her work load. Pa came upstairs and asked Lois and me to help Aunt Anna. My father's decision to leave placed extra housekeeping burdens on my Aunt Anna and Uncle Joe. I gradually saw over the years, growing up there, how we needed to depend on each other and help each other. Ironically, my father's leaving brought about a very happy childhood for me.

I know that some people think my mother had to be partly responsible for my father leaving. Maybe so, but I'm sure that neither my sister nor I did anything to cause him to leave. Billy wasn't even born yet. What about my father's responsibility as a parent? My mother taught me about responsibility as a parent, and she was a positive example of how to treat people.

My religion has been my lifeline in more ways than one. Besides the many benefits I receive from all of the religious services, there is a social aspect as well. I made the church my second home. I enjoyed all that the church offered, from my childhood to my now elderly age. I started with Holy Redeemer and then moved on to Our Lady of Perpetual Help. Now I go to St. John of Rochester. All of the gifted priests at these churches have given me great leadership in my faith. They have helped me when I was down without even knowing they helped me.

My aspirations continue on through my family, and I hope for the world to live in peace and with contentment. I know there are hard times. I've been there. For me, it was faith that helped me through. I held on to hope. I guess I wish that for everyone.

My goals are to continue to take care of my own health and to be the kind of person someone likes to stop in and visit. I welcome my family and friends anytime. I like to think that I can still help out in some way for someone in need, and I hope that everyone remembers to give back without always being a taker.

A favorite expression of mine is to bloom where you are planted. I try to follow that. I would like to be remembered as a fair and honest woman. I often ask myself what I have learned in my twilight years and how I can help those who come after me. No one really learns until the very end, and then no one really wants to hear what you have to say. I rec-ognize that people have to experience their own journey, but this old lady has some knowledge that perhaps others can benefit from.

Basically, it is quite simple. Love one another, even when it's hard to love one another. I still believe in doing unto others. Care. Help where you can. Please, stop in and talk. Share who you are and what you think and feel. A visit to neighbors doesn't seem to happen too much anymore. It seems that either the TV is on, or else there is some type of activity. My generation would have time to just sit and visit. I always enjoy playing a game, but I do miss just plain old conversation over a cup of tea.

While writing this memoir, I realized there are things I could have known. I wish I had had a loving father. I remember how my uncle Joe was to Helen, how she always got a special gift from him at Christmas. I wish Mom, Lois, Bill, and I could have had our own family home. Then Aunt Anna and Uncle Joe would have had their own home too. I wish there had not been so much drinking. I wish I could have passed on my faith, especially to my children.

And, without hesitation, there are so many experiences and people for which I am grateful. I am grateful for my sister, Lois, and my cousin Bob (we three are the last from 987). I thank God for the perseverance in my belief in the promises He has made (for God can neither "deceive nor be deceived")[3]; my ability to go to church and enjoy the services;

---

3 O my God, I firmly believe that you are one God in three divine persons, Father, Son and Holy Spirit. I believe that your divine Son became man and died for our sins, and that he will come to judge the living and the dead. I believe these and all the truths which the holy Catholic Church teaches, because in revealing them you can neither deceive nor be deceived.

my good health into old age (where I am only responsible for and to myself); my ability to have raised my children, seeing them grow to adulthood and enjoying the wonderful people they have become (they have given me five grandchildren and twelve great-grandchildren to know and love); and finally, to have learned to entrust everything to the Lord.

CPSIA information can be obtained at www.ICGtesting.com
Printed in the USA
BVOW11s1900081215

429777BV00017B/384/P